I0711386

Maple Leaf Language: Eh to Z

Toque

The toque, pronounced as "tuke," is a quintessential piece of Canadian winter attire. It's a knitted hat, typically made of wool or other warm materials, designed to keep the head and ears cozy during the frigid Canadian winters. The toque's origins can be traced back to French Canadian culture, where it was traditionally worn by French fur traders and settlers to protect them from the harsh winter elements of the Canadian wilderness.

Over time, the toque became a staple accessory for all Canadians, regardless of their heritage or geographical location. Its simple yet functional design makes it a practical choice for outdoor activities like skiing, snowboarding, and ice skating. Additionally, the toque has also become a fashion statement, with various styles, colors, and designs available to suit individual tastes.

Beyond its practical use, the toque holds cultural significance in Canada, symbolizing resilience, warmth, and a connection to the great outdoors. Whether worn atop a mountain peak or while strolling through a snowy city street, the toque is a symbol of Canadian identity and the enduring spirit of its people, embracing winter with warmth and style.

Double-double

A "double-double" is a cup of coffee with two creams and two sugars added to it. The name "double-double" stems from the doubling of both cream and sugar in the coffee, creating a rich and sweet beverage that's favored by many Canadians.

This unique coffee order has become deeply ingrained in Canadian culture and is often used as a symbol of national identity. Ordering a "double-double" at Tim Hortons is a ritual for many Canadians, whether they're grabbing a coffee on their way to work, during a road trip, or as a social gathering spot with friends and family. The familiarity and comfort of a "double-double" coffee reflect the warmth and hospitality associated with Canadian culture.

Beyond its literal meaning, the term "double-double" has also found its way into Canadian slang and colloquial language, often used to represent anything that comes in pairs or with extra flavor or sweetness. It serves as a reminder of the simple pleasures and shared experiences that bring Canadians together, one cup of coffee at a time.

Eh

"Eh" is an iconic interjection that is deeply ingrained in Canadian speech patterns and cultural identity. It is often used as a conversational filler or a tag question at the end of a sentence, similar to the English "right?" or "don't you think?" However, its usage extends beyond just seeking agreement; it can also be used to confirm information, prompt a response, or express surprise or disbelief.

The origins of "eh" are somewhat unclear, but it is believed to have originated from Scottish and Irish immigrants who settled in Canada in the 18th and 19th centuries. Over time, it became a prominent feature of

Canadian English, reflecting the country's multicultural heritage and linguistic influences. Today, "eh" is widely recognized as a quintessentially Canadian expression, often used affectionately by Canadians and stereotypically associated with Canadian speech patterns.

Despite its seemingly simple nature, "eh" plays a significant role in Canadian communication, serving as a marker of Canadian identity and fostering a sense of camaraderie and inclusivity among Canadians. It is a versatile and distinctive linguistic feature that embodies the friendly and laid-back demeanor for which Canadians are known worldwide. Whether used in casual conversation or as a playful nod to Canadian culture, "eh" is a beloved and enduring aspect of the Canadian linguistic landscape.

Loonie and Toonie

"Loonie" and "Toonie" are colloquial terms used in Canada to refer to the one-dollar and two-dollar coins, respectively. The term "Loonie" derives from the common loon, a bird featured on the reverse side of the one-dollar coin since its introduction in 1987. Similarly, "Toonie" is a portmanteau of "two" and "loonie," reflecting the two-dollar coin's status as the successor to the one-dollar coin.

The introduction of the Loonie in 1987 marked a significant shift in Canada's currency, as it replaced the one-dollar banknote. The decision to feature the iconic loon on the coin was influenced by its widespread recognition and association with Canadian wilderness and wildlife. The Toonie followed suit in 1996, featuring a polar bear on its reverse side and providing Canadians with a convenient and durable alternative to paper currency.

Today, the Loonie and Toonie are integral parts of everyday transactions in Canada, used in conjunction with coins and banknotes of other denominations. They have become symbols of Canadian identity and pride, reflecting the country's rich natural heritage and cultural diversity. The convenience and durability of these coins make them practical and enduring elements of Canada's monetary system, embodying the spirit of innovation and resilience that defines the nation.

Canuck

"Canuck" is a colloquial term used to refer to a Canadian person. It is often used informally and affectionately, similar to other national demonyms like "Yank" for Americans or "Aussie" for Australians. The origins of the term "Canuck" are somewhat unclear, but it is believed to have originated in the late 19th or early 20th century, possibly derived from the French-Canadian term "Canadien."

Over time, "Canuck" has become a widely recognized and accepted term for Canadians, both within the country and abroad. It is often used in informal settings, such as casual conversations, sports commentary, and media headlines. In some contexts, "Canuck" may also carry connotations of Canadian identity, culture, and values, evoking images of friendly, resilient, and multicultural people.

Despite its informal nature, "Canuck" holds a special place in Canadian vernacular and national pride. It is used to foster a sense of camaraderie and solidarity among Canadians, regardless of their background or geographical location. Whether used in jest, affection, or as a badge of identity, "Canuck" embodies the spirit of inclusivity and unity that characterizes Canadian society.

Poutine

Poutine is a quintessential Canadian dish that originated in the province of Quebec. It consists of a base of crispy French fries topped with cheese curds and smothered in rich, savory gravy. The dish is known for its indulgent and comforting flavors, making it a beloved staple of Canadian cuisine.

The exact origins of poutine are debated, but it is widely believed to have emerged in rural Quebec in the late 1950s or early 1960s. Some stories attribute its creation to a restaurant in Warwick, Quebec, while others claim it originated in Drummondville or Victoriaville. Regardless of its precise origins, poutine quickly gained popularity across

Quebec and eventually spread to other parts of Canada and the world.

Today, poutine is enjoyed by Canadians of all backgrounds and is served in a variety of settings, from casual diners and fast-food chains to upscale restaurants and food trucks. It has also inspired countless variations and creative interpretations, with toppings ranging from pulled pork and bacon to lobster and foie gras. Poutine has become synonymous with Canadian culinary identity and is celebrated as a delicious and indulgent comfort food that brings people together.

Hoser

"Hoser" is a slang term used primarily in Canada, especially in regions like Ontario and Western Canada, to refer to someone perceived as awkward, foolish, or unsophisticated. The term is often used in a lighthearted or playful manner and is typically associated with stereotypes of Canadian culture, such as ice hockey, beer drinking, and a love for the outdoors.

The origins of the term "hoser" can be traced back to Canadian ice hockey culture, where it was initially used to describe a player who frequently made mistakes or was considered inferior by their teammates. Over time, the term evolved to encompass a broader range of meanings, including someone who is clumsy, incompetent, or socially awkward.

Despite its negative connotations, "hoser" is often used affectionately among friends or as a form of playful teasing. It has also been embraced as a symbol of Canadian identity and is sometimes used ironically or nostalgically to evoke a sense of camaraderie and shared cultural heritage. While its usage may vary depending on context and region, "hoser" remains a distinctive and enduring aspect of Canadian slang.

Runners

"Runners" is a term commonly used in Canadian English to refer to athletic footwear, particularly sports shoes or sneakers. The term is widely understood across Canada and is used in both casual and formal contexts to describe shoes designed for running, jogging, or other physical activities.

The term "runners" reflects the practical and functional nature of athletic footwear, emphasizing their suitability for activities that involve running or fast movement. While the term is primarily used in Canada, it is also understood in other English-speaking countries, though it may not be as commonly used or as widely recognized.

"Runners" play an essential role in Canadian culture, particularly in outdoor activities like hiking, jogging, and playing sports such as basketball, soccer, and hockey. They are also a fashion staple, often worn as casual everyday footwear for their comfort and versatility. Whether hitting the trails or exploring the city streets, Canadians rely on their trusty "runners" to keep them comfortable and stylish on the go.

Mountie

"Mountie" is a colloquial term used to refer to a member of the Royal Canadian Mounted Police (RCMP), one of Canada's national police forces. The term is derived from the distinctive red serge uniform worn by RCMP officers, which includes a wide-brimmed Stetson hat, a scarlet tunic, and riding breeches with a stripe down the side.

The RCMP was established in 1873 as the North-West Mounted Police (NWMP) to maintain law and order in the western territories of Canada. Over the years, it evolved into the RCMP and expanded its jurisdiction to encompass all of Canada, serving as both a federal and provincial police force.

Mounties are iconic symbols of Canadian culture and law enforcement, known for their professionalism, dedication, and commitment to serving communities across the country. They undertake a wide range of duties, including enforcing federal laws, conducting criminal investigations, providing security services, and participating in search and rescue operations. Mounties are also recognized for their role in promoting Canadian values and heritage, both domestically and internationally. Whether on horseback, in patrol cars, or on foot, Mounties uphold the proud traditions of the RCMP and contribute to the safety and

security of Canadians from
coast to coast.

Chinook

A Chinook is a warm, dry wind that occasionally blows over the Canadian Rockies, particularly in the province of Alberta. This weather phenomenon can cause a rapid increase in temperature and can lead to the melting of snow and ice, even during the winter months. The term "Chinook" is derived from the Chinookan people of the Pacific Northwest, although the wind itself is not exclusive to that region.

Chinooks are often welcomed by residents of Alberta, especially during the winter, as they provide relief from the cold temperatures and heavy snowfall. The sudden warm spell can lead to dramatic changes in weather conditions, with temperatures rising by several degrees Celsius within a short period. This can result in the rapid thawing of frozen surfaces, including roads and sidewalks, and may cause flooding in some areas.

In addition to their practical implications for weather and climate, Chinooks hold cultural significance for residents of Alberta and other parts of Western Canada. They are the subject of folklore and legend, with stories passed down through generations about the mysterious and powerful nature of these warm winds. Chinooks are also celebrated for their role in enabling outdoor activities and providing a temporary reprieve from the harsh winter conditions that characterize much of Canada's interior.

Toonerville Trolley

The Toonerville Trolley is a nostalgic term referring to a fictional, rustic streetcar or tramway, often depicted in comic strips and cartoons from the early to mid-20th century. The name "Toonerville" suggests a whimsical and idyllic small town setting, evoking images of quaint neighborhoods, charming characters, and leisurely rides on the trolley.

The Toonerville Trolley gained popularity through the comic strip "Toonerville Folks," created by cartoonist Fontaine Fox in 1908. The strip featured a cast of eccentric characters living in the fictional town of "Toonerville," where the rickety trolley served as the primary mode of transportation. The adventures and misadventures of the trolley's passengers and crew provided humorous and heartwarming entertainment for readers.

While the Toonerville Trolley is a fictional creation, it has become a nostalgic symbol of a bygone era, reminiscent of simpler times and small-town charm. The phrase "Toonerville Trolley" is sometimes used colloquially to refer to any old-fashioned or antiquated mode of public transportation, serving as a whimsical reminder of the past. Despite its fictional origins, the Toonerville Trolley continues to capture the imagination of audiences, transporting them to a world of timeless humor and classic Americana.

Chesterfield

A Chesterfield is a type of upholstered sofa or couch that is characterized by its deep button-tufted upholstery, rolled arms, and often elaborate woodwork or detailing. The term "Chesterfield" is commonly used in Canada to refer to this style of sofa, while in other English-speaking countries it may be known by different names such as "sofa" or "couch."

The Chesterfield sofa has a rich history dating back to the 18th century, where it originated in England. It was named after the Earl of Chesterfield, a British nobleman who commissioned the first known design of this type of sofa. The Chesterfield quickly gained popularity among the English aristocracy and became associated with luxury, comfort, and sophistication.

In Canada, the term "Chesterfield" is still widely used to describe any sofa or couch, regardless of its specific design or style. While the traditional Chesterfield sofa may have fallen out of fashion in some regions, its name remains ingrained in Canadian English and is often used interchangeably with other terms for seating furniture. Whether used in casual conversation or formal settings, "Chesterfield" evokes a sense of timeless elegance and refinement, reflecting its prestigious origins and enduring appeal.

All-dressed

"All-dressed" is a term commonly used in Canadian English to describe a style of pizza or potato chips that are topped or flavored with a combination of various ingredients. The term originated in Quebec and has since become popular across Canada, particularly in the context of fast food and snack foods.

In the context of pizza, an "all-dressed" pizza typically includes a variety of toppings such as pepperoni, mushrooms, onions, green peppers, and sometimes additional ingredients like bacon, sausage, or olives. This combination of toppings offers a flavorful and satisfying experience that appeals to a wide range of tastes.

Similarly, "all-dressed" potato chips are flavored with a blend of seasonings that may include salt, vinegar, barbecue, sour cream and onion, and other savory flavors. This creates a bold and savory snack that combines the best of different taste profiles, making it a popular choice for chip enthusiasts across Canada. Whether enjoyed as a meal or a snack, "all-dressed" offerings are beloved for their versatility, flavor, and ability to satisfy cravings for savory indulgence.

Two-four

"Two-four" is a Canadian term used to refer to a case of 24 beers, typically sold in a single package. The term derives from the combination of the numbers "two" and "four," representing the quantity of beers contained within the case. "Two-four" is commonly used in Canada, especially during discussions about purchasing or consuming beer in bulk.

The term "two-four" holds cultural significance in Canada, particularly in the context of social gatherings, parties, and long weekends, such as Victoria Day or Canada Day. It is often associated with outdoor activities, barbecues, and cottage trips, where friends and family come together to relax and enjoy each other's company while sharing a case of beer.

While "two-four" originally referred specifically to cases of beer, it has since become a colloquial term used to describe any case or package containing 24 items of a particular product. This could include other beverages, such as soft drinks or bottled water, as well as non-beverage items like snacks or household goods. In Canadian vernacular, "two-four" is synonymous with convenience and camaraderie, representing the spirit of celebration and togetherness that defines Canadian social culture.

Caesar

The Caesar is a popular Canadian cocktail that is similar to the Bloody Mary but made with clamato juice instead of tomato juice. It typically consists of vodka, clamato juice (a blend of clam and tomato juices), hot sauce, Worcestershire sauce, and a variety of garnishes such as celery, olives, pickles, and lime wedges. The Caesar is known for its savory and refreshing flavor profile, making it a favorite choice for brunch or social gatherings.

The Caesar was invented in 1969 by bartender Walter Chell at the Westin Hotel in Calgary, Alberta. Inspired by the flavors of spaghetti alle vongole, an Italian pasta dish made with clams, Chell sought to create a unique cocktail that would appeal to his customers. The Caesar quickly gained popularity in Canada and has since become an iconic Canadian cocktail, enjoyed by millions across the country.

The Caesar holds a special place in Canadian culture and is often considered the unofficial national cocktail of Canada. It is commonly served in bars, restaurants, and social gatherings throughout the country, particularly during brunch or sporting events. The Caesar has also inspired numerous variations and adaptations, with bartenders and enthusiasts experimenting with different ingredients and garnishes to put their own spin on this beloved Canadian classic. Whether enjoyed on a patio in the summer or at a cozy bar in the winter, the Caesar remains a symbol of Canadian hospitality and culinary innovation.

Hydro

"Hydro" is a colloquial term used in Canada to refer to hydroelectric power, hydroelectricity, or the utility company responsible for providing electricity and water services in a specific region. The term "hydro" is derived from "hydroelectric," which describes the generation of electricity through the use of water, typically in the form of flowing or falling water.

In Canada, many provinces have publicly-owned or government-regulated utility companies that provide hydroelectric power to residents and businesses. These companies are responsible for generating electricity from hydroelectric dams, managing water resources, distributing electricity through power lines, and ensuring the reliability and safety of the electrical grid.

The term "hydro" is often used informally in conversations about energy consumption, utility bills, and environmental sustainability. Canadians may refer to their electricity bill as their "hydro bill" or discuss the benefits of "going hydro" by using renewable energy sources such as hydroelectric power. Hydroelectricity plays a significant role in Canada's energy landscape, providing clean and renewable energy to millions of people while reducing reliance on fossil fuels and mitigating the impacts of climate change.

Cheque

A cheque, spelled "check" in American English, is a written order directing a bank to pay a specific sum of money from the writer's account to the person or entity named on the cheque. Cheques are a common form of payment used in financial transactions, allowing individuals and businesses to make payments without the need for cash or electronic transfers.

To write a cheque, the account holder fills out the cheque form, including the payee's name, the amount to be paid in both numeric and written form, the date, and the signature of the account holder. The cheque is then presented to the payee, who can deposit or cash it at their bank. Cheques may also include additional information such as a memo line for specifying the purpose of the payment.

Despite advancements in electronic payment methods such as credit cards, debit cards, and online banking, cheques remain a widely used form of payment in many countries, including Canada. They are particularly favored for transactions involving larger sums of money, recurring payments, or situations where electronic payments are not feasible. While the use of cheques has declined in recent years, they continue to play an important role in commerce and finance, offering a convenient and secure means of

transferring funds between
individuals and businesses.

Molson muscle

"Molson muscle" is a humorous colloquial term used in Canada to refer to the beer belly or protruding abdomen that some individuals develop as a result of regularly consuming beer, particularly Molson beer. The term is a playful nod to the popular Molson Brewery, one of Canada's oldest and most well-known beer producers, and the tendency of beer drinkers to accumulate excess weight, especially around the midsection.

The term "Molson muscle" is often used in a light-hearted or self-deprecating manner, acknowledging the potential consequences of excessive beer consumption on one's physical appearance. It is sometimes employed in social settings or conversations about drinking habits, health, and fitness, serving as a humorous way to acknowledge the indulgences of Canadian beer culture.

While "Molson muscle" is primarily used in jest, it also reflects broader societal attitudes towards alcohol consumption and its effects on the body. Excessive beer consumption can contribute to weight gain and other health issues, and the term serves as a humorous reminder to drink responsibly and maintain a balanced lifestyle. Despite its humorous connotations, "Molson muscle" underscores the importance of moderation and mindfulness when it comes to alcohol consumption and overall health.

Kerfuffle

"Kerfuffle" is a whimsical and colorful term used to describe a commotion, disturbance, or fuss, often of a trivial or inconsequential nature. The word has its origins in Scottish and northern English dialects, where it originally referred to a disorderly or confused situation. Today, "kerfuffle" is commonly used in informal English to add flair and expressiveness to descriptions of minor disruptions or disagreements.

A kerfuffle may arise in various contexts, such as a heated argument, a misunderstanding, or a minor altercation. It can also refer to a noisy or chaotic situation, such as a crowded event or a bustling marketplace. Despite its lighthearted and somewhat humorous connotations, a kerfuffle can sometimes escalate into a more serious conflict if not addressed or resolved promptly.

The term "kerfuffle" is often used with a sense of amusement or irony, acknowledging the triviality or absurdity of the situation at hand. It is frequently employed in casual conversation, storytelling, and media headlines to describe incidents that are noteworthy for their drama or absurdity. Whether used to describe a minor spat between friends or a larger-scale controversy, "kerfuffle" adds a touch of whimsy and charm to everyday language, making it a favorite

among writers, speakers, and
storytellers alike.

Garburator

"Garburator" is a Canadian term used to describe a kitchen appliance known more commonly in other regions as a garbage disposal unit or garbage disposer. The garburator is typically installed beneath a kitchen sink and is designed to shred food waste into small particles, which can then be safely flushed down the drain with water.

The primary function of a garburator is to reduce the amount of organic waste that ends up in landfills by disposing of it through the sewer system. Food scraps such as vegetable peelings, fruit rinds, and leftover meals can be placed in the sink and ground up by the garburator, eliminating the need for separate food waste bins and reducing odors and pests in the kitchen.

Garburators are commonly found in Canadian households, where they are valued for their convenience and environmental benefits. However, they require proper use and maintenance to prevent clogs and damage to plumbing systems. Users should avoid putting non-food items, grease, oil, or large bones down the garburator, as these can cause blockages or mechanical failures. With proper care, a garburator can be a useful addition to a kitchen, helping to streamline meal cleanup and reduce household waste.

Pop

In Canada, "pop" is a widely used term for a carbonated soft drink, known as "soda" in the United States and various other terms around the world. It refers to beverages that are flavored and sweetened, typically with added carbonation for fizziness. Popular examples of pop brands include Coca-Cola, Pepsi, Sprite, and Mountain Dew.

The term "pop" is believed to have originated from the sound made when opening a carbonated beverage, which produces a popping noise as pressure is released from the bottle or can. In Canadian English, "pop" is the preferred term for soft drinks in many regions, though variations such as "soda" or "soda pop" may also be used in certain areas.

Pop is a ubiquitous beverage in Canada, enjoyed by people of all ages and consumed in various settings, including homes, restaurants, movie theaters, and parties. It comes in a wide range of flavors and varieties, from classic cola to fruit-flavored sodas and diet options. While preferences may vary regionally, pop remains a popular choice for quenching thirst and satisfying cravings for something sweet and refreshing.

Two-four

"Two-four" is a colloquial term used in Canada to refer to a case of 24 beers, typically sold in a single package. The term "two-four" is derived from the combination of the numbers "two" and "four," representing the quantity of beers contained within the case. It is a common expression used in Canadian English, particularly in discussions about purchasing or consuming beer in bulk.

Two-fours are a popular choice for social gatherings, parties, and long weekends, such as Victoria Day or Canada Day, where friends and family come together to celebrate and relax. They are often associated with outdoor activities, barbecues, and cottage trips, where sharing a case of beer is a common tradition.

While "two-four" originally referred specifically to cases of beer, the term has since become a colloquial expression used to describe any case or package containing 24 items of a particular product. This could include other beverages, such as soft drinks or bottled water, as well as non-beverage items like snacks or household goods. In Canadian vernacular, "two-four" is synonymous with convenience and camaraderie, representing the spirit of celebration and togetherness that defines Canadian social culture.

Keener

In Canadian English, a "keener" is a term used to describe someone who is excessively eager, enthusiastic, or ambitious, especially in academic or extracurricular pursuits. The term carries both positive and negative connotations, depending on the context in which it is used.

Keeners are often characterized by their high level of motivation, diligence, and competitiveness, striving to excel academically, participate in numerous activities, and achieve recognition or success. They may be eager to answer questions in class, volunteer for additional responsibilities, or take on leadership roles in school or community organizations.

While keeners are admired for their dedication and ambition, they may also be perceived as overzealous or insincere by their peers, particularly if their enthusiasm comes across as obnoxious or competitive. The term "keener" is often used informally in Canadian schools and universities to describe students who are perceived as overly eager or try-hard, sometimes in a teasing or derogatory manner. Despite its mixed reputation, being a keener can be a source of pride for individuals who value academic and personal achievement, embodying the spirit of determination and perseverance.

The 6ix

"The 6ix" is a colloquial term used to refer to the city of Toronto, Ontario, Canada. The term is derived from the city's area code, 416, which covers much of the Greater Toronto Area (GTA). It has become a popular nickname and cultural identifier for Toronto, embraced by residents, visitors, and celebrities alike.

The term "The 6ix" gained widespread popularity after being popularized by Toronto-born rapper Drake, who frequently refers to the city by this nickname in his music and public appearances. It has since become a symbol of pride and identity for Torontonians, representing the city's diversity, creativity, and vibrancy.

"The 6ix" is often used in a variety of contexts, including social media hashtags, event promotions, and colloquial conversations. It encompasses the diverse neighborhoods, cultures, and attractions that make Toronto unique, from its bustling downtown core to its vibrant arts and entertainment scene. Whether used by locals or visitors, "The 6ix" captures the essence of Toronto as a dynamic and cosmopolitan city, continually evolving and embracing its rich multicultural heritage.

Parkade

A "parkade" is a multi-level parking structure or parking garage commonly found in urban areas, shopping centers, office complexes, and other locations where parking space is limited. The term "parkade" is primarily used in Canadian English, while similar structures in other regions may be referred to as parking garages, parking decks, or parking structures.

Parkades typically consist of multiple levels or floors equipped with ramps, elevators, and stairwells for vehicles to access and navigate between parking spaces. They are designed to maximize parking capacity in a limited footprint, allowing drivers to park their vehicles securely and conveniently while minimizing the use of valuable land space.

Parkades offer a convenient parking solution for commuters, shoppers, and visitors to urban areas, providing a safe and sheltered environment to park vehicles away from the elements. They may also feature amenities such as security cameras, lighting, and payment systems to enhance safety and convenience for users. In dense urban environments where street parking is scarce, parkades play a crucial role in alleviating parking congestion and supporting economic activity by providing accessible parking options for drivers.

Homo milk

"Homo milk" is a colloquial term used in Canada to refer to homogenized milk, a type of dairy product that has undergone a process called homogenization. Homogenized milk is the most common type of milk found in grocery stores and supermarkets across Canada and is widely consumed by Canadians of all ages.

Homogenized milk is produced by blending milk from multiple cows and then subjecting it to a mechanical process that breaks down the fat molecules into smaller particles. This process prevents the cream from separating and rising to the top of the milk, resulting in a uniform consistency throughout the product. As a result, homogenized milk has a smooth and creamy texture that is preferred by many consumers.

"Homo milk" is a staple in Canadian households, used for drinking, cooking, baking, and other culinary purposes. It is available in various fat percentages, including whole (3.25% milk fat), 2% reduced-fat, 1% low-fat, and skim (fat-free) options, to accommodate different dietary preferences and nutritional needs. Whether enjoyed in a bowl of cereal, a cup of coffee, or a creamy sauce, homo milk is cherished for its rich flavor and versatility in everyday cooking and dining.

Klick

"Klick" is a military slang term used in Canada to refer to a distance of one kilometer (or approximately 0.62 miles). The term originated from military jargon and is commonly used by members of the Canadian Armed Forces as well as civilians with military backgrounds.

In military contexts, precise communication of distance is essential for coordinating operations, planning maneuvers, and assessing terrain. The use of standardized units such as the kilometer (klick) allows for clear and efficient communication among personnel in various branches and units of the military.

Outside of military circles, "klick" may occasionally be used informally by Canadians to refer to a distance of one kilometer in everyday conversation. While less common in civilian contexts, the term may be employed casually or humorously to convey distance, particularly in outdoor activities such as hiking, running, or cycling. Overall, "klick" serves as a shorthand for expressing distance, rooted in military tradition and occasionally adopted in civilian vernacular.

KD (Kraft Dinner)

"KD," short for "Kraft Dinner," is a popular brand of packaged macaroni and cheese dinners produced by Kraft Heinz Canada. It is one of Canada's most iconic and beloved convenience foods, known for its quick preparation, cheesy flavor, and affordability.

KD typically consists of dried pasta noodles and a powdered cheese sauce mix, which are cooked separately and then combined to create a creamy and flavorful dish. The product is a staple in Canadian households, particularly among students, busy families, and budget-conscious consumers seeking a quick and satisfying meal option.

In addition to its convenience and affordability, KD holds a special place in Canadian culture as a nostalgic comfort food and symbol of childhood. Many Canadians have fond memories of enjoying KD as a quick and easy meal during their formative years. The distinctive bright orange color of the cheese sauce and the familiar "KD" logo are instantly recognizable to generations of Canadians. Overall, KD remains a beloved Canadian culinary institution, cherished for its simplicity, convenience, and nostalgic appeal.

Beauty

"Beauty" is a term often used colloquially in Canadian English to describe something or someone that is visually appealing, attractive, or pleasing to the senses. While the concept of beauty is subjective and can vary greatly depending on individual preferences and cultural norms, it generally refers to qualities that evoke admiration, appreciation, or admiration.

Beauty can be found in various forms, including natural landscapes, works of art, human faces, and expressions of creativity. It may encompass physical attributes such as symmetry, proportion, and harmony, as well as intangible qualities such as grace, elegance, and charisma. Beauty is often associated with feelings of joy, wonder, and awe, inspiring people to pause and appreciate the world around them.

In Canadian culture, the concept of beauty is celebrated and valued in diverse ways, reflecting the country's rich tapestry of landscapes, cultures, and traditions. From the majestic mountains of the Rockies to the vibrant urban skylines of Toronto and Vancouver, Canada offers an abundance of beauty to explore and experience. Whether found in the natural world or human creations, beauty serves as a source of inspiration, connection, and enrichment in Canadian life.

Gong show

"Gong Show" is a colloquial term used in Canadian English to describe a chaotic or disorganized situation, event, or performance. The term is derived from the popular television show "The Gong Show," which originally aired in the United States in the 1970s and featured amateur performers competing in often bizarre and outrageous acts.

In Canadian vernacular, "Gong Show" is used metaphorically to describe any situation that is characterized by confusion, disorder, or incompetence. It may refer to events such as meetings, gatherings, or projects that are poorly organized, mismanaged, or fraught with difficulties. The term is often employed humorously to convey a sense of frustration or exasperation with chaotic circumstances.

Despite its negative connotations, "Gong Show" can also be used affectionately to describe situations that are entertaining or memorable due to their unpredictability or absurdity. The term has become a colorful and expressive part of Canadian slang, evoking images of comedic mishaps, unexpected twists, and larger-than-life personalities. Overall, "Gong Show" serves as a playful and humorous way to describe the ups and downs of life's unpredictable moments.

Hang a Larry

"Hang a Larry" is a colloquial expression used predominantly in Canadian English to denote the action of making a left turn while driving. The term is informal and derives from the association of "Larry" with the direction left, while "hang" implies executing the turn in that direction.

In practical terms, "hanging a Larry" simply means steering the vehicle to the left side of the road, typically at an intersection or designated turning point, in order to change direction onto a perpendicular street or pathway. It's a common maneuver in everyday driving and is often accompanied by the use of a vehicle's turn signal to indicate the intention to turn left.

This expression is frequently used in casual conversation or when providing driving directions, adding a touch of colloquial flair to the act of making a left turn. While light-hearted and informal, "Hang a Larry" serves as a vivid and memorable way to convey the action of turning left while driving, making it a distinctive feature of Canadian English vernacular.

Twoonie

A "twoonie" is a colloquial term used in Canada to refer to the Canadian two-dollar coin. The name "twoonie" is a portmanteau of "two" and "loonie," the latter being a common nickname for the one-dollar coin in Canada.

The twoonie features a distinctive bi-metallic design, with a bronze-colored outer ring and a silver-colored center. It was introduced by the Royal Canadian Mint in 1996 as a replacement for the two-dollar banknote. The coin is circular in shape, with a diameter of 28 millimeters, and is adorned with various designs and motifs, including the Canadian national emblem, the maple leaf.

The twoonie is widely used in everyday transactions throughout Canada and is accepted as legal tender alongside other Canadian coins and banknotes. It has become an iconic symbol of Canadian currency and is recognized and valued by Canadians across the country. The term "twoonie" is commonly used in casual conversation and financial transactions, reflecting the coin's significance in Canadian monetary culture.

Sled

A "sled" is a vehicle designed for traveling over snow or ice, typically consisting of a flat-bottomed platform or frame mounted on runners or skis. Sleds are used for various purposes, including transportation, recreation, and sport, and come in a variety of shapes, sizes, and designs to suit different needs and preferences.

Traditional sleds are often made of wood and feature simple construction, with curved runners or skis attached to the underside to glide smoothly over snow or ice. More modern sleds may be constructed from materials such as plastic, metal, or fiberglass, offering increased durability, stability, and maneuverability.

Sleds are commonly used for activities such as sledding, tobogganing, and ice fishing, providing hours of outdoor enjoyment for people of all ages, particularly in regions with snowy winters. They may also be used for practical purposes, such as hauling goods or equipment over snow-covered terrain. Overall, sleds are versatile and beloved vehicles that play an important role in winter recreation and transportation in many parts of the world.

Bunnyhug

"Bunnyhug" is a unique term used in Saskatchewan, Canada, to describe a type of hooded sweatshirt or hoodie. The term "bunnyhug" is specific to the province and is not commonly used in other regions of Canada or elsewhere.

A bunnyhug typically features a hood, long sleeves, and a front kangaroo pocket, similar to other hooded sweatshirts. However, what distinguishes a bunnyhug is its regional name and the cultural significance it holds for Saskatchewan residents. The term "bunnyhug" is believed to have originated from the action of hugging oneself while wearing the garment, resembling the way a bunny (rabbit) might hug with its front legs.

Bunnyhugs are popular casual attire in Saskatchewan and are worn by people of all ages and backgrounds, especially during the colder months. They provide warmth and comfort while also showcasing a sense of regional pride and identity. The term "bunnyhug" reflects the unique linguistic and cultural heritage of Saskatchewan and is a cherished part of the province's vernacular.

Housecoat

A "housecoat" is a loose-fitting garment worn by individuals, typically women, for comfort and modesty within the confines of their home. Also known as a "dressing gown" or "robe," the housecoat is designed to be worn over sleepwear or regular clothing and provides warmth and coverage while lounging or performing household tasks.

Housecoats are often made from soft, comfortable fabrics such as cotton, flannel, or terry cloth, and may feature a wrap-around or button-up design for easy wear. They come in various lengths, ranging from knee-length to ankle-length, and may include additional features such as pockets, belts, or decorative trims.

In Canadian culture, the term "housecoat" is commonly used to refer to this type of garment, particularly in English-speaking regions of the country. Housecoats are a practical and versatile wardrobe staple, providing both comfort and functionality for everyday wear around the house. Whether worn while enjoying a morning cup of coffee, getting ready for bed, or relaxing after a long day, the housecoat is a cozy and familiar presence in many Canadian households.

Biff

"Biff" is a slang term used in Canadian English to describe a physical altercation or fight between individuals. It is typically used informally and may be employed to describe a variety of confrontations, ranging from minor scuffles to more serious altercations.

The term "biff" can be used as a verb to describe the action of engaging in a fight or altercation ("to biff someone"), or as a noun to refer to the altercation itself ("getting into a biff"). It is often used in casual conversation or informal settings, particularly among friends or peers.

While the term "biff" is primarily used in Canadian

English, it may also be understood in other English-speaking regions, albeit less commonly. It is a colorful and expressive word that conveys the idea of physical conflict in a straightforward and often humorous manner. Overall, "biff" serves as a vivid and memorable descriptor for moments of interpersonal conflict or confrontation.

Deke

"Deke" is a slang term primarily used in ice hockey, particularly in Canada, to describe a deceptive move or feint made by a player to evade an opponent or goalie. The term is short for "decoy" and is commonly used to refer to maneuvers that involve quickly changing direction or faking out an opponent in order to gain a tactical advantage.

In ice hockey, a deke typically involves the use of quick footwork, body fakes, or stickhandling skills to maneuver past an opposing player or goalie. Players may use dekes to create scoring opportunities, evade defenders, or maintain possession of the puck during gameplay. Dekes are often executed with speed, precision, and finesse, making them a key aspect of offensive strategy in hockey.

The term "deke" is widely recognized and understood within the hockey community, both in Canada and internationally. It is a fundamental skill for players at all levels of the game, from amateur to professional, and is often practiced and perfected through drills and training exercises. The ability to execute effective dekes can significantly impact a player's success on the ice, making it an important aspect of hockey strategy and gameplay.

Buck

"Buck" is a colloquial term used in Canadian English to refer to a dollar. The term is derived from the historical use of animal skins, particularly deer or buckskins, as a form of currency in early North American trade. Over time, "buck" became synonymous with the dollar and is now commonly used in everyday language to denote currency in Canada.

In modern usage, "buck" is often used informally to refer to a single dollar bill or coin. It may also be used more broadly to describe any denomination of currency, particularly when discussing monetary amounts in casual conversation or slang expressions. For example,

someone might say they paid
"ten bucks" for a coffee, meaning
they paid ten dollars.

The term "buck" is deeply
ingrained in Canadian
vernacular and is widely
understood across the country.
It is a versatile and familiar
term that adds color and
character to everyday
language, particularly when
discussing financial matters or
making casual references to
money. Overall, "buck" serves as
a convenient shorthand for
referring to currency in
Canadian English.

Chirping

"Chirping" is a slang term commonly used in Canadian English, particularly in the context of sports, to describe the act of taunting, teasing, or engaging in friendly banter with opponents or teammates. The term derives from the idea of making light, playful remarks akin to the sound of birds chirping.

In sports, chirping often occurs during games or competitions, where players engage in verbal sparring or good-natured trash talk to psych out their opponents or build camaraderie with teammates. Chirping can range from harmless jokes and witty remarks to more pointed comments aimed at getting under the skin of opponents.

Chirping is considered a common and accepted part of sports culture in Canada, particularly in hockey and lacrosse, where it is seen as a way to assert dominance, boost team morale, and add excitement to the game. While chirping can sometimes escalate into more heated exchanges, it is generally viewed as a lighthearted and entertaining aspect of competitive sportsmanship. Overall, chirping adds an element of fun and camaraderie to the sporting experience, fostering a sense of camaraderie and camaraderie among players and fans alike.

Loonie bin

"Loonie bin" is a humorous term used in Canadian English to describe a designated container or receptacle where loose one-dollar coins, commonly known as "loonies," are collected or stored. The term is a playful play on words, combining "loonie" with "bin" to create a whimsical and memorable expression.

In practical terms, a loonie bin may be any container or vessel, such as a jar, box, piggy bank, or bowl, used to gather and organize loose change, specifically one-dollar coins. It serves as a convenient and centralized location for individuals to deposit their spare change, whether for personal saving, group fundraising, or charitable donations.

The term "loonie bin" is often used humorously or informally in everyday conversation, particularly when discussing the management or organization of loose change. It reflects the quirky and creative nature of Canadian English, where wordplay and humor are common features of language. Additionally, the use of "loonie" emphasizes the cultural significance of the iconic Canadian coin, which features a common loon, a bird native to Canada, on its reverse side. Overall, "loonie bin" serves as a colorful and memorable expression that adds a touch of whimsy to discussions about currency and saving.

Gitch

"Gitch" is a colloquial term used in Canadian English to refer to men's underwear, particularly briefs or boxer briefs. The term is informal and is primarily used in casual conversation or among close friends in a humorous or lighthearted context.

The origin of the term "gitch" is uncertain, but it likely stems from a regional or dialectical variation of the word "get," possibly influenced by other slang terms for underwear. It is a playful and affectionate term that adds a touch of humor to discussions about undergarments.

In practical terms, "gitch" is synonymous with men's

underwear and is often used interchangeably with other terms such as "undies," "boxers," or "briefs." While the term may not be widely recognized outside of Canada, it is a familiar and beloved part of Canadian vernacular, reflecting the country's unique linguistic quirks and cultural identity. Overall, "gitch" is a colorful and expressive word that adds character to conversations about men's clothing and personal hygiene.

Toonie Tuesday

"Toonie Tuesday" is a promotional event or special offer that occurs on Tuesdays, particularly in Canadian businesses such as restaurants, movie theaters, or retail stores. The term "toonie" refers to the Canadian two-dollar coin, which features a polar bear on its reverse side, and "Tuesday" signifies the day of the week when the promotion takes place.

During Toonie Tuesday, businesses may offer discounts, deals, or special pricing on their products or services to attract customers and boost sales. For example, restaurants might offer discounted meals, movie theaters might offer reduced-price tickets, or retail stores might offer buy-one-get-one-free deals on certain items.

Toonie Tuesday is a popular and widely recognized concept in Canada, known for providing consumers with opportunities to save money and enjoy value-priced offerings. It has become a regular fixture in many Canadians' calendars, with people actively seeking out Toonie Tuesday deals as a way to stretch their budgets and indulge in affordable treats or experiences. Overall, Toonie Tuesday reflects the ingenuity of businesses in attracting customers and the enthusiasm of consumers in taking advantage of savings and bargains.

Hogtown

"Hogtown" is a colloquial nickname for the city of Toronto, Ontario, Canada. The term dates back to the late 19th and early 20th centuries when Toronto was known for its thriving meatpacking industry and large number of slaughterhouses, which led to the city being associated with the processing of pork, or "hog."

Despite its origins in Toronto's industrial past, the term "Hogtown" has endured and become a beloved and enduring nickname for the city. It is often used affectionately by residents and visitors alike, reflecting Toronto's rich history, cultural diversity, and vibrant urban landscape.

Today, Hogtown is synonymous with Toronto's dynamic and bustling cityscape, renowned for its arts and culture scene, culinary offerings, sports teams, and iconic landmarks such as the CN Tower and Royal Ontario Museum. While the city has evolved and transformed over the years, the nickname "Hogtown" serves as a nostalgic reminder of Toronto's heritage and resilience, capturing the spirit and character of Canada's largest metropolis.

Brown bread

"Brown bread" refers to a type of bread that is made with whole wheat flour or a mixture of whole wheat and white flours. Unlike white bread, which is made from refined flour that has been stripped of its bran and germ, brown bread retains these nutritious components, giving it a darker color and denser texture.

Brown bread is prized for its health benefits, as it is higher in fiber, vitamins, and minerals compared to white bread. The inclusion of whole grains in brown bread provides essential nutrients and promotes digestive health, making it a popular choice among health-conscious consumers.

In addition to its nutritional value, brown bread is valued for its hearty flavor and satisfying texture. It can be enjoyed in various forms, including sliced loaves, rolls, buns, and artisanal varieties. Brown bread is a versatile staple in many cuisines around the world, used for sandwiches, toast, accompaniments to soups and stews, and as a base for savory and sweet dishes alike. Overall, brown bread is celebrated for its wholesome ingredients, robust flavor, and contributions to a balanced and nutritious diet.

Screech-in

"Screech-in" is a traditional Newfoundland ceremony or ritual that is often performed to welcome newcomers to the province or to honor visitors to Newfoundland and Labrador. The term "screech" refers to a type of rum that is closely associated with Newfoundland, particularly the brand known as "Newfoundland Screech."

During a screech-in ceremony, participants gather in a social setting, often at a pub, bar, or community event, where they engage in a series of humorous and lighthearted rituals. The ceremony typically involves the recitation of a scripted oath or pledge, the consumption of screech rum, and the kissing of a codfish, which is a symbolic gesture of becoming an honorary Newfoundlander.

Screech-ins are steeped in Newfoundland folklore and tradition, reflecting the province's rich maritime heritage, cultural pride, and sense of camaraderie. While the specific details of a screech-in may vary depending on the host and participants, the ceremony is always characterized by its jovial and welcoming atmosphere, as well as its celebration of Newfoundland identity and hospitality. Overall, a screech-in is a memorable and cherished experience for both locals and visitors alike, fostering connections and forging bonds within the close-knit communities of Newfoundland and Labrador.

Run a tab

"Run a tab" is a colloquial expression used in the hospitality industry, particularly in bars, pubs, and restaurants, to refer to the practice of allowing customers to accumulate charges for their purchases over multiple visits rather than paying immediately for each transaction.

When a customer runs a tab, they provide their name or a unique identifier to the establishment, and their orders are recorded by the staff throughout their visit. At the end of the visit or upon request, the customer settles their bill in full, paying for all of their accumulated purchases at once.

Running a tab is a convenient and common practice for both customers and establishments, as it allows patrons to enjoy their experience without the hassle of paying after each transaction, while also encouraging repeat business and fostering customer loyalty. However, it requires trust and responsibility on the part of both the customer and the establishment to ensure that all charges are accurately recorded and settled in a timely manner. Overall, running a tab is a flexible and customer-friendly approach to managing transactions in the hospitality industry, enhancing the overall experience for all parties involved.